I WONDER WHY THE WIND BLOWS?

MOONSTONE

PUBLISHED IN MOONSTONE
BY RUPA PUBLICATIONS INDIA PVT. LTD 2026
161-B/4, GULMOHAR HOUSE,
YUSUF SARAI COMMUNITY CENTRE,
NEW DELHI 110049

SALES CENTRES:
BENGALURU CHENNAI
HYDERABAD KOLKATA MUMBAI

P-ISBN: 978-93-7003-674-1
E-ISBN: 978-93-7003-515-7
FIRST IMPRESSION 2026

10 9 8 7 6 5 4 3 2 1

PRINTED IN INDIA

Table Of Contents

What Is Wind?

Is wind invisible?

YES, WIND IS MOVING AIR. ALTHOUGH WE CAN'T SEE IT, WE FEEL IT BRUSHING AGAINST OUR CHEEKS, SEE IT RIPPLE ACROSS WATER, AND HEAR IT WHISTLING THROUGH WINDOWS AND TREES.

Where does wind come from?

THE SUN WARMS EARTH UNEVENLY, HEATING LAND, WATER, AND AIR DIFFERENTLY. WARM AIR RISES, COOLER AIR SINKS, AND THIS RESTLESS SHIFTING CREATES THE INVISIBLE CURRENTS WE CALL WIND.

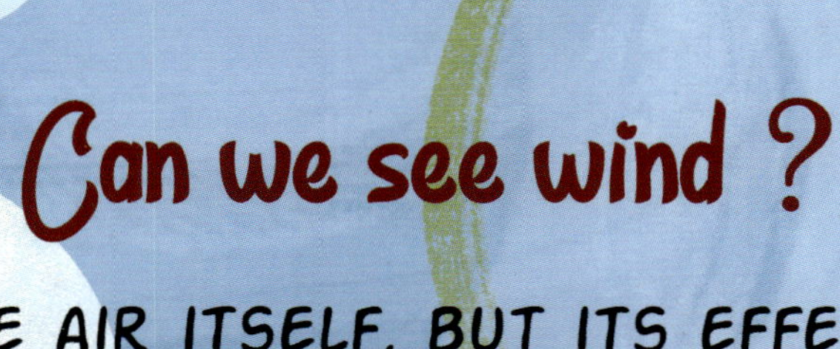

Can we see wind ?

NOT THE AIR ITSELF, BUT ITS EFFECTS ARE EVERYWHERE—WASHING FLAPS ON LINES, FLOWERS NOD, WAVES SWELL, AND DANDELION SEEDS SPIN. WIND LEAVES A VISIBLE TRAIL WHEREVER IT TRAVELS.

Does wind have strength ?

YES. A LIGHT BREEZE FEELS GENTLE AND PLAYFUL, WHILE A GALE CAN KNOCK BRANCHES DOWN. WINDS CAN COOL US, CARRY RAIN, OR SHAPE LANDSCAPES, DEPENDING ON THEIR SPEED AND POWER.

Why Does Air Move ?

Why does hot air rise ?

WHEN AIR WARMS, ITS PARTICLES SPREAD APART AND GROW LIGHTER. RISING UPWARD, IT LEAVES SPACE BEHIND, WHICH COOLER, HEAVIER AIR RUSHES TO FILL–CREATING THE CYCLE THAT MOVES OUR ATMOSPHERE.

What happens to cool air ?

COOL AIR IS HEAVY, SO IT SINKS. AS IT FALLS, IT PUSHES INTO SPACES LEFT BY RISING WARM AIR. THIS CONSTANT MOVEMENT OF SWAPPING CREATES BREEZES AND GUSTS EVERYWHERE.

Does this make wind ?

YES. THE RISE OF WARM AIR AND FALL OF COOLER AIR POWER MOST WINDS. THE GREATER THE TEMPERATURE DIFFERENCE, THE STRONGER AND FASTER THE MOVEMENT BECOMES ACROSS LAND AND SEA.

Where does it happen ?

EVERYWHERE! FROM MOUNTAIN SLOPES TO SANDY BEACHES, AIR IS CONSTANTLY RISING, SINKING, AND FLOWING. EVEN IN YOUR BACK GARDEN, LITTLE AIR CURRENTS DRIFT SILENTLY AROUND YOU EACH DAY.

Does the Sun Make Wind?

How can sunshine make air move?

THE SUN DOESN'T HEAT EVERY SURFACE EVENLY. LAND WARMS QUICKLY, WATER WARMS SLOWLY, AND AIR CHANGES IN BETWEEN. THESE DIFFERENCES SET AIR MOVING, CREATING THE WINDS THAT SWEEP OUR PLANET.

Is it hotter by day?

YES. BY DAY, SUNSHINE HEATS THE LAND, MAKING WARM AIR RISE. BY NIGHT, THE LAND COOLS FASTER THAN THE SEA, AND THE DIRECTION OF THE BREEZES SWITCHES COMPLETELY AROUND.

So without the sun would we have wind ?

NO. THE SUN IS THE ENGINE BEHIND EVERY BREEZE. WITHOUT ITS WARMTH TO SET AIR RISING AND FALLING, OUR WORLD WOULD BE STILL, SILENT, AND WINDLESS FOREVER.

What about oceans?

OCEANS KEEP THEIR WARMTH LONGER THAN LAND. ON HOT AFTERNOONS, COOLER SEA AIR BLOWS INLAND AS A REFRESHING BREEZE. AT NIGHT, THE PROCESS REVERSES AND AIR FLOWS BACK OUT.

Why Does Wind Change Direction?

Does wind always blow the same way?

NO. WINDS SHIFT DIRECTION AS TEMPERATURES AND PRESSURES CHANGE. THAT'S WHY WE MAY WAKE TO A BREEZE FROM THE WEST, BUT BY AFTERNOON IT HAS TURNED TO THE EAST.

What is air pressure?

AIR MAY BE INVISIBLE, BUT IT HAS WEIGHT. WHEN IT PRESSES HEAVILY, IT'S CALLED HIGH PRESSURE. WHEN IT PRESSES LIGHTLY, WE CALL IT LOW PRESSURE. WINDS FORM BETWEEN THEM.

How does it move air ?

AIR NATURALLY FLOWS FROM HIGH PRESSURE TO LOW PRESSURE, JUST LIKE WATER RUNNING DOWNHILL. THIS SIMPLE MOVEMENT SPREADS ACROSS THE GLOBE, DRIVING THE BREEZES AND GALES WE EXPERIENCE DAILY.

Can we predict the wind ?

YES. METEOROLOGISTS WATCH PRESSURE MAPS, USE BALLOONS, AND TRACK SATELLITES. THEIR FORECASTS WARN US WHERE WINDS WILL TRAVEL, WHETHER THEY'LL BE GENTLE BREEZES OR FIERCE STORMS ARRIVING SOON.

Why Do We Name Winds ?

Do special winds have names ?

YES. REGULAR WINDS HAVE BEEN GIVEN NAMES. MONSOONS BRING SEASONAL RAIN IN ASIA, MISTRALS SWEEP COLD THROUGH FRANCE, AND CHINOOKS MELT CANADIAN SNOW WITH SURPRISING BURSTS OF WARM AIR.

Why name them ?

BECAUSE THESE WINDS ARE PART OF PEOPLE'S LIVES. BY NAMING THEM, COMMUNITIES COULD SHARE WARNINGS, CELEBRATE THEIR ARRIVAL, OR PREPARE FOR THE CHALLENGES AND BLESSINGS EACH WIND MIGHT BRING.

Are all winds the same temperature?

NO. SOME BLOW ICY AND SHARP, STINGING OUR SKIN. OTHERS ARRIVE HOT AND DRY, SWEEPING ACROSS DESERTS. WINDS CARRY THE CHARACTER OF THE REGIONS THEY COME FROM WITH THEM.

Do winds bring rain too ?

YES. WINDS OVER OCEANS SOAK UP WATER VAPOUR. WHEN THE MOIST AIR COOLS AND RISES, CLOUDS FORM. SOON, RAINDROPS FALL, WATERING FIELDS, FILLING RIVERS, AND FEEDING PLANTS EVERYWHERE.

What Are Storm Winds ?

Are storms just strong winds ?

YES, BUT THEY ARE WINDS PUSHED TO EXTREMES. THEY CAN UPROOT TREES, SMASH WINDOWS, AND RAISE WAVES HIGHER THAN HOUSES. THEIR POWER COMES FROM RAPIDLY RISING AND SINKING AIR.

What's a hurricane ?

A HURRICANE IS A GIANT WHIRLING STORM THAT FORMS OVER WARM SEAS. IT SPINS ACROSS OCEANS, CARRYING HEAVY RAIN, FIERCE WINDS, AND FLOODING WAVES THAT REACH FAR INLAND.

What about a tornado?

A TORNADO IS SMALLER BUT EVEN MORE INTENSE. IT LOOKS LIKE A TWISTING FUNNEL CLOUD, ROARING ACROSS LAND. ITS WINDS ARE SO STRONG THEY CAN LIFT CARS AND TEAR HOUSES APART.

Which is strongest?

TORNADOES HAVE THE FASTEST WINDS, BUT HURRICANES LAST LONGER AND COVER GREATER DISTANCES. BOTH REMIND US HOW MIGHTY AND DANGEROUS MOVING AIR CAN BE WHEN NATURE STIRS IT VIOLENTLY.

Can Wind Travel Far?

Does wind stay in one place?

NO, WINDS CAN CROSS OCEANS AND CONTINENTS. A STORM THAT BEGINS IN ONE PART OF THE WORLD MAY CARRY ITS AIR THOUSANDS OF KILOMETRES BEFORE FINALLY SLOWING DOWN.

Can it carry things?

YES, WIND IS A NATURAL CARRIER. IT PICKS UP DUST, GRAINS OF SAND, TINY INSECTS, AND LIGHT SEEDS, CARRYING THEM ACROSS DISTANCES. SOME SEEDS TRAVEL MILES BEFORE TOUCHING GROUND.

Is that helpful ?

YES, WINDS HELP PLANTS SPREAD TO NEW PLACES, MOVING SOIL, SHAPING DUNES, AND MIXING AIR. WITHOUT WIND, MANY ECOSYSTEMS WOULD NEVER HAVE GROWN AS WIDELY AS THEY DO.

Is it harmful too ?

SOMETIMES. DUST STORMS CAN COVER VILLAGES, WILDFIRES SPREAD QUICKLY WITH STRONG WINDS, AND STORMS DAMAGE CROPS. WINDS ARE USEFUL, BUT THEY CAN ALSO CAUSE DANGER WHEN THEY GROW FIERCE.

Can We Use Wind ?

What did people use wind for ?

FOR CENTURIES, WIND POWERED SAILING SHIPS ACROSS SEAS AND OCEANS. WINDMILLS ALSO HARNESSED BREEZES TO GRIND GRAIN, PUMP WATER, AND HELP COMMUNITIES SURVIVE IN WINDY LANDS.

Do we still use it ?

YES. WE BUILD WIND TURBINES THAT SPIN IN BREEZY FIELDS OR OFFSHORE. THEY TURN AIR'S ENERGY INTO ELECTRICITY, POWERING HOMES, SCHOOLS, AND EVEN WHOLE TOWNS WITH CLEAN STRENGTH.

Can wind power whole towns ?

YES. COUNTRIES WITH STRONG WINDS BUILD LARGE WIND FARMS. TOGETHER, THE TURBINES PRODUCE ENOUGH ELECTRICITY TO LIGHT CITIES, RUN TRAINS, AND POWER FACTORIES WITHOUT HARMING THE ENVIRONMENT.

Is wind energy clean?

YES. UNLIKE BURNING COAL OR OIL, WIND ENERGY DOESN'T RELEASE SMOKE OR POLLUTION. IT IS RENEWABLE, MEANING IT NEVER RUNS OUT, AS LONG AS THE SUN KEEPS SHINING.

Why Do Mountains Make Wind?

Do hills change the wind?

YES. WIND SPEEDS UP WHEN SQUEEZED THROUGH VALLEYS. IT WHISTLES THROUGH GAPS, RUSHES DOWN SLOPES, AND SOMETIMES GROWS STRONG ENOUGH TO MAKE MOUNTAIN PASSES DANGEROUS FOR TRAVELLERS.

What happens on mountainsides?

DURING THE DAY, SUNSHINE HEATS SLOPES, LIFTING AIR UPWARDS. AT NIGHT, THE SLOPES COOL, AND AIR SLIDES BACK DOWN. THIS DAILY RHYTHM CREATES MOUNTAIN BREEZES AND SHIFTING VALLEY WINDS.

Do mountain winds matter ?

YES. THEY CARRY SNOW, HELP FORM STORMS, AND SOMETIMES BRING CLEAR, FRESH AIR. FARMERS, HIKERS, AND ANIMALS ALL ADAPT TO THESE CHANGING WINDS HIGH IN THE MOUNTAINS.

Can climbers feel it ?

ABSOLUTELY. AT THE TOP OF MOUNTAINS, THERE'S LITTLE TO BLOCK THE AIR. CLIMBERS OFTEN BATTLE STRONG WINDS, CLINGING TO ROPES OR SHELTERS AS BREEZES ROAR ALL AROUND THEM.

Do Winds Shape Our World?

Can wind change landscapes?

YES, OVER TIME WINDS WEAR DOWN ROCK, CARVE ARCHES, AND SHAPE CLIFFS. IN DESERTS, THEY CREATE RIPPLING DUNES THAT STRETCH FOR MILES, REARRANGING THE SURFACE OF THE EARTH.

Does it make deserts?

NOT ALONE, BUT WINDS HELP THEM GROW. THEY CARRY GRAINS OF SAND, PILING THEM INTO DUNES, OR SWEEPING THEM INTO WAVES THAT ROLL ACROSS THE BARREN DESERT FLOOR.

Does wind shape coasts too ?

YES, SEA BREEZES PUSH WAVES THAT GRIND AWAY CLIFFS, FORM SANDY BEACHES, OR MOVE PEBBLES. WINDS WORK WITH WATER TO SCULPT COASTLINES OVER MANY YEARS AND CENTURIES.

Can wind make music ?

YES! AIR WHISTLES THROUGH CAVES, SINGS IN CHIMNEY POTS, AND HOWLS IN STORMS. SOME INSTRUMENTS, LIKE PANPIPES OR FLUTES, ARE DESIGNED TO LET THE WIND'S VOICE BECOME MUSIC.

How Do We Measure Wind?

Can we see how fast it blows?

YES. ANEMOMETERS MEASURE SPEED BY SPINNING IN THE AIR. THE FASTER THEY TURN, THE STRONGER THE WIND IS BLOWING ACROSS THE LANDSCAPE AROUND THEM.

How do we tell direction?

WEATHER VANES, SHAPED LIKE ARROWS OR ROOSTERS, POINT IN THE DIRECTION WIND IS COMING FROM. WATCHING THEM TURN ON ROOFTOPS SHOWS WHICH WAY THE AIR IS FLOWING.

Do we measure strength too ?

YES. SAILORS ONCE CREATED THE BEAUFORT SCALE TO DESCRIBE WINDS, FROM A GENTLE BREEZE THAT STIRS LEAVES TO A VIOLENT STORM STRONG ENOUGH TO TOPPLE TREES.

Why measure it ?

SO WE CAN FORECAST WEATHER, PREPARE FOR STORMS, AND PLAN SAFELY. KNOWING WIND SPEED HELPS SHIPS SAIL, PLANES FLY, AND BUILDERS KEEP CRANES STEADY IN STRONG GUSTS.

Why Is Wind Important for Animals ?

Do animals use wind ?

YES. BIRDS GLIDE ON RISING AIR CURRENTS, SAVING THEIR ENERGY. SOME EVEN TRAVEL THOUSANDS OF MILES, LIFTED BY WINDS THAT CARRY THEM ACROSS OCEANS AND CONTINENTS.

What about insects ?

MANY INSECTS, LIKE BUTTERFLIES, DRAGONFLIES, AND EVEN TINY SPIDERS, DRIFT ON BREEZES. SOME SPECIES RELEASE SILK THREADS TO CATCH THE WIND, FLOATING LIKE PARACHUTES THROUGH THE AIR.

Do fish notice wind ?

YES, BECAUSE WINDS STIR THE OCEANS. THEY CHURN UP NUTRIENTS, PUSHING FOOD CLOSER TO THE SURFACE, WHERE FISH GATHER TO FEED. WITHOUT WINDS, OCEANS WOULD BE FAR LESS LIVELY.

Can animals smell scents on the wind ?

YES. WOLVES, DOGS, AND MOTHS FOLLOW SMELLS DRIFTING ON AIR CURRENTS. A SINGLE GUST CAN CARRY THE SCENT OF FOOD, FLOWERS, OR DANGER FROM FAR AWAY.

Are There Winds in Space ?

Is there air in space ?

NO, SPACE IS A VACUUM, WITH ALMOST NO AIR. BUT STARS LIKE OUR SUN STILL RELEASE STREAMS OF TINY PARTICLES RACING THROUGH SPACE AT HIGH SPEEDS.

What does solar wind do ?

SOLAR WIND CAN STRIKE EARTH'S ATMOSPHERE, CAUSING AURORAS—DANCING LIGHTS THAT SHIMMER GREEN, RED, AND PURPLE NEAR THE NORTH AND SOUTH POLES. THEY ARE THE SKY'S MOST MAGICAL DISPLAY.

Can solar wind harm us ?

USUALLY NOT. EARTH'S MAGNETIC FIELD SHIELDS US FROM MOST OF IT. VERY STRONG BURSTS, THOUGH, CAN DISRUPT SATELLITES AND EVEN AFFECT ELECTRICITY GRIDS ON THE GROUND.

Do other planets have winds ?

YES. GAS GIANTS LIKE JUPITER AND NEPTUNE HAVE STORMS WITH WINDS FAR FASTER THAN EARTH'S. NEPTUNE'S WINDS HOWL AT SPEEDS OVER 2,000 KILOMETRES AN HOUR!

Will the Wind Always Blow?

Will wind ever stop?

NO. AS LONG AS THE SUN KEEPS SHINING, EARTH'S SURFACE WILL HEAT UNEVENLY, AIR WILL KEEP RISING AND SINKING, AND WINDS WILL CONTINUE TO STIR THE ATMOSPHERE.

Can we run out of wind energy?

NO. WIND ENERGY IS RENEWABLE. UNLIKE FUELS THAT BURN AWAY, BREEZES NEVER RUN OUT. THEY WILL CONTINUE AS LONG AS EARTH ORBITS THE SUN AND AIR KEEPS MOVING.

Does every place have wind?

YES, THOUGH NOT EQUALLY. COASTLINES, PLAINS, AND MOUNTAINS ARE BREEZIER, WHILE FORESTS AND CITIES MAY BLOCK OR SLOW THE AIR. BUT EVERYWHERE FEELS A GUST NOW AND AGAIN.

Will Earth always need wind ?

YES. WINDS MOVE CLOUDS, SPREAD SEEDS, GUIDE ANIMALS, AND BALANCE EARTH'S WEATHER. WITHOUT THEM, AIR WOULD GROW STAGNANT, AND LIFE AS WE KNOW IT COULD NOT THRIVE.

A mini quiz :

What causes air to rise and sink, creating wind ?

____

What tool measures how fast wind is blowing ?

____

What creates the dazzling auroras in the night sky ?

____

How do seeds and insects sometimes travel across great distances ?

____